Find a Career
That Fits You

Leanne Currie-McGhee

San Diego, CA

For more information, contact:
ReferencePoint Press, Inc.
PO Box 27779
San Diego, CA 92198
www.ReferencePointPress.com

LIBRARY OF CONGRESS CATALOGING-IN-PUBLICATION DATA

Names: Currie-McGhee, Leanne, 1971- author
Title: Find a career that fits you / by Leanne Currie-McGhee.
Description: San Diego, CA : ReferencePoint Press, Inc, 2026. | Includes bibliographical references and index.
Identifiers: LCCN 2025006175 (print) | LCCN 2025006176 (ebook) | ISBN 9781678210809 library binding | ISBN 9781678210816 ebook
Subjects: LCSH: Teenagers--Vocational guidance--Juvenile literature | Vocational guidance--Juvenile literature | Occupations--Juvenile literature | Job hunting--Juvenile literature
Classification: LCC HF5381.2 .C873 2026 (print) | LCC HF5381.2 (ebook) | DDC 650.140835--dc23/eng/20250418
LC record available at https://lccn.loc.gov/2025006175
LC ebook record available at https://lccn.loc.gov/2025006176

CONTENTS

Building Your Future

As a teenager, deciding what to do with your life can seem overwhelming. Some young people, like sixteen-year-old Kavya Kopparapu, are lucky enough to find and build on their passions early in life. While still in high school, Kopparapu led her school's bioinformatics society, organized a research symposium, played the piano, and attended computer programming workshops. While she enjoyed all of these activities, she found herself increasingly drawn to projects involving technology and computer skills.

When Kopparapu's grandfather developed diabetic retinopathy, a complication of diabetes that damages blood vessels in the retina, she decided to pursue this area for research. Along with her younger brother and a high school classmate, Kopparapu trained an artificial intelligence (AI) system to recognize signs of diabetic retinopathy in photos of eyes and offer a preliminary diagnosis. They turned this into a smartphone app called Eyeagnosis. When paired with a 3-D-printed lens, the app transforms the diagnostic procedure from a two-hour exam to a quick photo taken with a phone.

While working on this project and others, Kopparapu says, she realized that she had a passion for putting her scientific skills and knowledge to practical use. "It's one thing to go to school, learn something and just leave it at that," she says. "But it's another thing to enjoy it . . . and apply it in the real world."[1] Kopparapu went on to study computer science at Harvard University. After graduating in 2022, she began her career as a research engineer at DeepMind, a

Google-affiliated AI research laboratory. She also founded the Girls Computing League, a nonprofit organization dedicated to improving student access to emerging technology education.

Not all teens will discover their passion and travel a direct path to a career, as Kopparapu did. Many will need time and real-world experiences to find their way. Whether you already know what interests you or are still figuring it out, experts suggest taking time to explore your interests and passions as a means to understanding yourself and shaping your future.

Exploring Careers Early On

The teen years are ideal for career exploration, offering a unique chance to learn about and engage in activities related to various fields. Even if you do not have a clear vision of your future, experimenting with potential career areas can help you discover what excites you, feels meaningful, and suits the skills you already have or the skills you want to acquire. This can be done in various ways, including through classes, volunteer work, or extracurricular activities. Discovering these insights early, rather than waiting until later, enables you to make informed choices in school and in life.

> **"They may not realize it, but by waiting until those later years to start career exploration, they've already limited their options and potential."[2]**
>
> —Katherine Kemmeries Cecala, president of the Arizona chapter of Junior Achievement

Katherine Kemmeries Cecala explains that early exposure to different careers helps teens expand their options. Cecala is president of the Arizona chapter of Junior Achievement (JA), a nonprofit organization that works with young people on financial literacy, career readiness, and entrepreneurship. "They may not realize it, but by waiting until those later years to start career exploration, they've already limited their options and potential," she says. "Almost like a form of tunnel vision, they may focus solely on the ideas and opportunities directly in front of them at that time."[2] By looking into different options as a teen, you are less likely to merely end up in a career as opposed to actively finding one that aligns with your interests.

A high schooler participates in an ornamental plaster demonstration at a Junior Achievement career expo in Rock Island, Illinois.

Early career exploration can have a lasting impact. A 2022 survey by the Ipsos polling organization found that 81 percent of adults who had participated in JA's programs as young students felt that the experience positively influenced their career and education decisions. Additionally, 90 percent said that JA enhanced their motivation to learn and increased their belief in their own potential. This reveals that even small steps in career exploration can lead toward future success.

Connecting Your Passions to a Purpose

Exploring different career options is not just about identifying job titles or salary levels—it is a journey to connect your interests, passions, and skills to a meaningful purpose. One of the best ways to start finding this connection is by diving deeper into the activities that you find most compelling. Volunteer, join clubs, and experiment with hobbies to discover what excites you. The key is to look for activities that make time fly by or spark curiosity, because they reveal the things you truly care about.

Dylan, a high school student at William Floyd High School in New York, discovered his interest in carpentry through a two-year carpentry program at his school. He also gained hands-on experience by volunteering with Habitat for Humanity, a nationwide nonprofit organization that builds homes for those in need. His school's partnership with Habitat for Humanity enables students to use their skills and help people at the same time. Dylan saw the positive impact of his work and appreciated the satisfaction it gave him. "Together, we replaced and rebuilt most of the house," Dylan says of one Habitat project he worked on. "We put down the plywood across the beams so we'd be able to walk around. We had to make a new deck, paint, lay new tile, buy new appliances, everything."[3] This work opened his eyes to a potential and, for him, fulfilling career in carpentry or construction. Connecting interests with a career path can make your hard work feel purposeful and give you satisfaction.

Setting Goals for the Future

The process of exploring potential careers and identifying interests can help teens stay motivated—in school and in other activities. A glimpse into future possibilities can make even the most challenging classes or tasks seem like steps toward a larger dream. Whether it is studying hard in biology for a medical career or learning carpentry as Dylan did to build houses, having a sense of purpose makes hard work feel more meaningful and rewarding. Ultimately, the path to discovering a fulfilling career is unique to each person, but by starting exploration as a teen, you can uncover more possibilities and find what excites you.

Understanding Yourself—Discovering Interests, Skills, and Values

Finding the right career starts with understanding who you are. It begins with uncovering your passions, identifying your talents, and recognizing what you value most. For teenagers, this stage is especially important because it lays the groundwork for decisions that shape their future. As you engage in this process, you will find that self-discovery is not always about finding a specific answer—it is often about the journey and what you learn about yourself along the way.

Self-Assessment: The Foundation of Career Planning

The first step in finding a career path is self-assessment. Understanding your personality, interests, and skills can provide a clearer direction for the future. To help gain that understanding, some students turn to career assessment tools. If one of these tools identifies an interest in environmental science, for instance, the student could expand on this interest by joining the school ecology club and later interning at a conservation organization. Both activities could help that student discover a passion for solving environmental issues.

There are several online self-assessment questionnaires. They typically take fifteen to thirty minutes to complete. The results show a person's likely personality type along with careers that might be interesting to that person. Tools like the Myers-Briggs Type Indicator (MBTI) and the Holland Code are among the many resources available for assessing personality and career possibilities. The MBTI categorizes individuals into personality types, helping them understand their strengths and how they interact with others. The Holland Code links specific interests—like artistic, investigative, or social tendencies—to compatible career environments.

Online self-assessment questionnaires show a person's likely personality type along with careers they might find interesting.

The insights gained from these tools can help teens identify the types of careers that might be a good fit for their personality and interests. One person describes the result of using an assessment tool at age nineteen:

> At the end of my sophomore year in college, I started to worry. Two of the most popular paths forward for philosophy majors—going to law school or entering a graduate program for philosophy—weren't appealing to me. I was pretty sure that I didn't want to be an attorney or a philosophy professor. At the time, all of my friends were lining up internships and making plans for grad school . . . and I felt completely lost.[4]

A career counselor suggested taking a self-assessment test. The test revealed an aptitude for marketing, a field the student had never considered. That revelation ultimately led to a fulfilling career, as the student explains:

> It stated marketing/advertising as an ideal match for me. . . . I had no exposure to business or marketing growing up—it was the antithesis of my artsy upbringing—so I had no idea what to expect. My knowledge of the field was limited to the episodes I had seen of *Mad Men*. Yet, I signed up for a course in marketing and applied for an internship at an advertising agency . . . and the rest is history. . . . I love what I do because I feel challenged every day at work, I get to work on projects that interest me, and I feel that I leverage my natural strengths. I feel extremely lucky that I've found my niche.[5]

Exploring Hobbies and Extracurriculars

While self-assessment tools can help identify strengths and interests, considering hobbies and other activities that you enjoy can

Gaining Skills

Participating in a club can help students discover or prepare for career paths that extend beyond the club's primary focus. The Distributive Education Clubs of America (DECA), for instance, does not always lead participants to business careers. The skills it teaches can be applied to a wide range of professions. Ilana Stein took part in DECA while in high school and then pursued an education major at Florida State University. She credits DECA with honing her writing and speaking abilities. "I have always been an advanced writer and have enjoyed the creative process. However, typing up a business plan that you have to create yourself is an entirely new monster that I had to explore and figure out. My DECA advisors . . . tore apart every draft of my papers and significantly improved my writing and on-paper presentation skills," she explains. Problem-solving and communication skills, foundational to her DECA experience, prepared Stein for both college and her future career in education.

Ilana Stein, "10 Things DECA Taught Me for the Real World," The Odyssey, March 25, 2019. www.theodysseyonline.com.

also provide a glimpse into potential career paths. For example, a love for gardening could inspire a career in horticulture or landscape design, while an interest in robotics might lead to an engineering career.

High school activities like clubs, sports, or volunteer work offer opportunities to develop skills while learning about yourself. This is why it is important to join clubs and participate in activities that spark your interest. Mackenzie Perez discovered her love for marketing through her involvement in the Distributive Education Clubs of America (DECA), a nonprofit organization that prepares high school and college students for careers in marketing, finance, hospitality, and management. Students participate in DECA clubs at their schools and engage in activities like creating business plans, solving case studies, and presenting marketing strategies to industry professionals. After being an active member throughout high school, Perez knew what her path should be when she started at Clemson University. "DECA introduced me to skills I never knew I had, and now I'm a marketing major at my dream university,"[6] Perez shares.

Even casual hobbies can lead to professional opportunities. Some of the teens who volunteer at Longwood Gardens

Hobbies and other activities can provide a glimpse into potential career paths. An interest in robotics, for instance, might lead to an engineering career.

in Pennsylvania just enjoy visiting the public botanical gardens. Others have a passion for plants, which they can indulge in the gardens' more than 1,100 acres (445 ha). Whatever their reasons for being there, teen volunteers gain hands-on experience with caring for plants and giving talks and tours to visitors. They also build connections with staff and other volunteers, opening doors to careers in horticulture, conservation, or environmental science.

Classes at school also provide opportunities to explore interests. Jake Christianson pursued his passion for photography by taking several arts classes in high school. "My school offered classes that allowed me to explore my interest in the arts, including videography and photography, and learn about topics of my choice,"[7] he writes. These classes helped him realize he wanted a career centered on photography. Deciding that college wasn't the right path for him, Christianson also focused on building his business skills during high school. A year after graduating in 2023, he was running his own photography and video production business.

"My school offered classes that allowed me to explore my interest in the arts, including videography and photography, and learn about topics of my choice."[7]

—Jake Christianson, photographer and videographer

Analyzing Strengths and Weaknesses

While finding your interests is important, determining your strengths and areas for improvement is equally valuable. Strengths are often easier to identify. Feedback from teachers, coaches, or friends can reveal talents that might otherwise go unnoticed. For example, a student recognized for leadership in group projects might consider a future in management or entrepreneurship.

Afaf Maliha, a MacArthur High School senior in Texas, discovered her strength in computer science during her sophomore year. Maliha initially had no interest in programming, but her mother urged her to take the AP Computer Science Principles class anyway. She did—and what she found surprised her. She actually liked the class, and she was good at it. Part of the class included designing an app. "When we started creating it, it was really fun to figure out the logic behind it all," says Maliha. "At first, I made a super long, complicated code, and then with the help of one of my classmates, we figured out how to shorten it. That was exciting for me because it all seemed very logical, like a puzzle."[8]

Path from High School to Congress

The path to finding a satisfying career does not always follow a straight line. It can take various turns, so it is important to stay open to and explore different options. Many people experience this. In high school Alexandria Ocasio-Cortez (now a US representative from New York) was passionate about science. She even competed in an international science and engineering fair. Years later her high school science teacher recalled that she was interested in using scientific research to help people live better, healthier, happier, more productive lives.

Over time her desire to help people evolved into an interest in economics and international relations. Ocasio-Cortez eventually chose a career in politics because she felt she could do the most good for the most people in this role. She was elected to Congress in 2018 at age twenty-nine. As a member of Congress, she has taken up causes that draw on her earlier interest in science, economics, and global relations. These causes include efforts to address climate change and advocating for programs that enhance public health.

> "Writing became my speech pathology. The more I recited, the better I became."[9]
>
> —Amanda Gorman, poet and speaker

Recognizing personal challenges can also provide valuable insights. Amanda Gorman, the poet who performed at President Joe Biden's 2021 inauguration, transformed a speech impediment into a source of strength. Diagnosed with an auditory processing disorder and struggling with speech issues as a child, Gorman practiced reciting poetry, spoken word, and rap to improve her pronunciation. Through this process, she discovered a love of poetry and became the first National Youth Poet Laureate in 2017. "Writing became my speech pathology. The more I recited, the better I became,"[9] she explains. Her determination not only improved her speech but also launched her career as a poet and public speaker.

Connecting Personal Values to Career Options

After identifying your interests, personality traits, strengths, and personal challenges, consider your values when thinking of potential career paths. What motivates you? What issues or causes do you care deeply about? Considering these questions can lead toward a fulfilling career.

Amanda Gorman reads a poem during the 59th Presidential Inauguration at the U.S. Capitol in Washington on January 20, 2021.

Values lay at the heart of Nupol Kiazolu's decision to become a civil rights activist. Kiazolu, of Brooklyn, New York, embarked on the road to activism at age twelve after the shooting death of Trayvon Martin in Florida in 2012. Martin, a seventeen-year-old African American high school student, was unarmed when he was fatally shot by a neighborhood watch volunteer. The shooter was charged with second-degree murder but claimed self-defense and was later acquitted. This decision sparked nationwide protests against racial injustice. It was then that Kiazolu knew she needed to become involved in this fight. Kiazolu has participated in other high-profile protests even while pursuing her degree in political science and prelaw at Hampton University. During the same time period, she became the president of the Black Lives Matter of Greater New York Youth Coalition and has received widespread recognition for her work, including being named to *Teen Vogue*'s 2018 "21 Under 21" list.

Since graduating from Hampton University in 2024, Kiazolu has worked as a civil rights activist and organizer. This includes founding and running We Protect Us, an organization aimed at empowering Black and Brown communities in New York. "We are not asking or waiting for change," Kiazolu says of her work. "We're taking it. The work I do in communities across the country affords me the opportunity to work closely with people at a grassroots level."[10]

Values can act as a guide, steering you toward careers that align with what matters most to you. For Kiazolu, her focus on civil rights has led her to a career of activism. If you value creativity, you might thrive in artistic fields such as graphic design or writing. If fairness is important, law or public policy could be a good fit. Start by creating a list of what you value most. Thinking about these priorities can help give you an idea of what careers might bring long-term satisfaction.

It is also important to know that values evolve over time. As you grow, your experiences will shape what you consider important.

Keeping an open mind ensures that your career journey remains flexible and aligned with your personal growth.

Be Open and Curious

A career journey is not about finding all the answers, particularly in high school. It is about staying open and actively engaging in new experiences so you can discover unexpected opportunities and interests. Upon graduating from Bronx High School of Science in 2023 and preparing to go to college, Sebastian Rosero-Mayer wrote that high school and college were about exploring the possibilities. "I've always wanted to be a journalist, so perhaps I write for my college's newspaper as I have in high school. Maybe I want to work as a financial advisor, or maybe even pursue something completely different such as becoming a lawyer," wrote Rosero-Mayer. "We do not have to have it all figured out at this stage of our lives. The journey of finding our true calling is often filled with twists, turns, and unexpected detours."[11]

"We do not have to have it all figured out at this stage of our lives. The journey of finding our true calling is often filled with twists, turns, and unexpected detours."[11]

—Sebastian Rosero-Mayer, 2023 high school graduate

Exploration is not meant to be a straight line to a chosen career. Try new activities, take different classes, meet people from different backgrounds, and learn about several careers you might not have considered. Every experience adds to your understanding of yourself, and that is what will help you find what you want in life. Starting this process in high school increases the chances you will find a path that excites you and feels worthwhile.

Research, Resources, and the Real World

Korey Busby wanted to create as many opportunities as possible for herself and made the most of her time at MacArthur High School in Houston to explore potential career paths. By joining clubs like the Black Student Union and the National Technical Honor Society, as well as taking center stage in the school play, she discovered a variety of interests that fueled her curiosity. However, it was her decision to dive into her school's career programs—particularly the medical courses, including an emergency medical technician class—that set her on the path toward a career in health care.

After graduating high school in 2018, Busby began her journey in the medical field by enrolling at the University of Virginia, where she chose to major in nursing with a minor in African American studies. Reflecting on her goals, Busby says, "Upon graduation, I would like to use the skills I have gained from both my majors to provide care to marginalized populations that have historically been neglected by the healthcare system."[12] By taking advantage of the career resources offered at her high school, Busby started building a foundation for her ambitions and future success.

"Upon graduation, I would like to use the skills I have gained from both my majors to provide care to marginalized populations that have historically been neglected by the healthcare system."[12]

—Korey Busby, University of Virginia nursing student

Finding Reliable Resources

While Busby's exploration of her school programs guided her toward a health care career, individual research is another way for high school students to explore future possibilities and build confidence. Knowledge Matters is an educational platform that offers interactive virtual business simulations to help high school and college students explore career paths and build critical professional skills. The platform points out that career exploration not only builds practical skills but also helps students understand their strengths and interests, ultimately enabling them to make informed decisions about their future.

One valuable resource for students is the online *Occupational Outlook Handbook*, created by the Bureau of Labor Statistics. The handbook provides essential details on hundreds of occupations, including responsibilities, average salaries, future outlook, and educational requirements. Additionally, the bureau's website has student-focused pages that offer articles and interviews that enhance career exploration.

Students can use a variety of online tools to help with their career research and planning. One such tool, the online Occupational Outlook Handbook*, provides details about pay, educational requirements, future outlook, and more in connection with hundreds of occupations.*

Another key tool is O*NET Online, a platform funded by the US Department of Labor. It offers extensive career profiles and allows users to explore jobs based on skills, interests, or industry demand. For example, students interested in creative careers can search for roles requiring artistic skills, while those leaning toward science, technology, engineering, and math (STEM) fields can explore in-demand technical careers.

For a closer look at real-world careers, students can turn to online platforms like LinkedIn and Monster. LinkedIn isn't just for professional networking; it also includes many industry insights, featuring professional profiles, career tips, and internship opportunities. Similarly, Monster provides detailed job descriptions, industry trends, and advice on résumés and interviews.

Resources like these can help students identify required skills and explore the options in various career fields. For example, discovering that a software developer typically needs a bachelor's degree in computer science and proficiency in programming languages like Python can guide a student to take relevant high school courses or join coding clubs. Additionally, understanding job outlook data can help students assess which industries are growing and align their goals accordingly. By using available tools, students can explore a wide range of careers and gain the clarity they need to make informed decisions about their future. With a little research, they can connect their skills and passions to real-world opportunities.

Firsthand Learning

Career exploration is not just about research—it is also about gaining firsthand experience. Internships, volunteer work, and part-time jobs offer invaluable opportunities to understand different career fields, develop practical skills, and build confidence. Experiencing a work environment allows students to discover their preferences and strengths.

> "Through internships, you'll see your strong points, which areas you might want to work on, and which are simply not for you."[13]
>
> —Laure Depaty, former sales and marketing intern

Laure Depaty was a student in the International Baccalaureate program at the Zurich International School, a private school in Switzerland known for its rigorous academic curriculum. Alongside her studies, she interned in the sales and marketing department of a large Swiss company. This internship experience gave her new insight into her own interests and strengths. "Find out what you like and dislike, it'll help when making decisions regarding which path you're interested in following," Depaty writes. "Through internships, you'll see your strong points, which areas you might want to work on, and which are simply not for you."[13]

By gaining real-world experience, students not only strengthen their résumés but also open doors to future opportunities. A report by the US Department of Labor revealed that 47 percent of college graduates who completed internships in their field of study received at least one job offer within six months of graduation. While this statistic applies to college students, high school internships can similarly enhance employability by providing valuable experience and skills.

High school students can start finding information about internships by speaking with school counselors, using job boards like Handshake, or exploring industry-specific websites. Andrew Cruz secured a summer internship at the defense and aerospace company Lockheed Martin before starting college

Mapping Your Career

There are many innovative online platforms that students can use to explore career possibilities. The nonprofit organization Roadtrip Nation offers one such tool on its website. You can go to the website and take a virtual road trip through a variety of different careers. On the website, you first answer three simple questions about your interests and goals. Based on the answers you give, you are introduced to various careers and stories about real people working in jobs in those career fields. The website also shows the connection between college majors and various jobs. Platforms like Roadtrip Nation give youth different ways of exploring future options.

Internships enhance employability by giving high schoolers the opportunity to gain valuable on-the-job experience and skills.

in 2023. His AP Computer Science teacher had encouraged him to join his school's computer science club. Cruz and other club members participated in the Code Quest competition, a regional coding contest sponsored by Lockheed Martin. The company offered internship applications to those who participated, and after applying and interviewing, Cruz's passion for computer science helped him land the internship. During his internship, Cruz learned and used new coding languages and gained valuable communication and teamwork skills. "The whole point of an internship is to learn and gain experience,"[14] Cruz says. Finding the work engaging, Cruz decided to pursue a combined math and computer science major at the University of California, Los Angeles.

Volunteer Opportunities and Part-Time Jobs

Volunteer work can also offer meaningful career exploration. Organizations like the Humane Society, Habitat for Humanity, and local food banks encourage participation by teen volunteers. As volunteers, teens can explore potential career paths while gaining valuable experience.

This was true for Nicole, who started volunteer work at the Ronald Reagan UCLA Medical Center when she was a sophomore in high school. This led her to explore her interest in the medical field and make contacts with people in that field. She started by working as a patient escort and eventually had the opportunity to volunteer in the neurobiology department. "Now in my junior year of college, I am grateful for the rewarding insight volunteering has given me into the medical field and the great networking opportunities that have led me into research. It has been a great experience volunteering, and I would highly recommend it to anyone interested in the health field or to anyone wanting to lend a helping hand,"[15] Nicole shares.

In addition to volunteering, part-time jobs can offer a chance to build connections and discover how one feels about different career fields. According to a Pew Research Center report, about 30 percent of US teens ages sixteen to nineteen hold part-time jobs, with many reporting that these experiences helped them develop confidence and discipline. While part-time jobs for high school students are often considered entry-level positions, they can also provide exposure to fields of interest. For example, a student aspiring to become a chef might work in a local restaurant to learn about the food industry, while someone interested in retail management could take a job at a clothing or sporting goods store.

First jobs can also teach soft skills, like teamwork, communication, and time management, that are essential in any career. Working as a ski instructor during the winter has provided valuable lessons for Ann of Glenbard West High School in Chicago. "During the wintertime, I work as a ski instructor at a local ski hill most days after school. It helps encourage me to be productive and also helps me understand time management and what having a job is like,"[16] she shares. This job has taught Ann how to work with children, become a better teacher, and adapt to different learning styles.

From Volunteer to Career

Johanna Kuehne's passion for animals began at a young age. When she was around nine years old, she started volunteering at an animal shelter. She continued to volunteer with animals throughout her youth, including assisting with fostering kittens. She bottle-fed and played with the kittens, which helped get them used to people in preparation for adoption. She loved working with the animals and knew this was her path.

Kuehne's volunteer experience helped her get her first job at a veterinary clinic while still in high school. Her job included basic lab work. She also observed surgeries. These opportunities solidified her desire to build a career working with animals. "By the time I was 18, I realized . . . I want to be working with animals, and I want to do this full time," Kuehne explains.

Following high school, she began working at the Grand Companions Humane Society in Fort Davis, Texas. As a medical coordinator assistant, she administers vaccinations, manages medical intake, and assists with various medical procedures. She recently enrolled in a two-year veterinary technologist program. Kuehne credits her volunteer work and her high school job with helping her find a career that fits her personality and interests.

Quoted in Roadtrip Nation, "What's Next After High School?," 2022. https://roadtripnation.com.

Internships, volunteer work, and part-time jobs provide high school students with real-world experience. These hands-on opportunities not only build skills but also help students find their passions, giving them a head start on learning what careers are possible.

School and Community Connections

Another valuable resource for career exploration is the counselors at most high schools. School counselors generally have information about programs and classes that students can use to learn about career options, explore their interests, and gain the skills they need for future success. Counselors may be able to offer career assessments, career days, résumé workshops, and job-shadowing opportunities that allow students to explore specific fields.

Counselors often have connections with local businesses and can help students secure internships or take part in career-related events. Errin Howard is the career opportunities program director for Inland Rivers, Ports & Terminals, a maritime industry trade association based in St. Louis, Missouri. Howard works closely with high school counselors to encourage young people to attend maritime industry career events. At these events, they have a chance to learn about careers they might never have known existed.

Summer Programs

Summer programs are another resource for high school students looking to explore career fields. Many colleges, universities, and community organizations offer summer opportunities that allow students to gain hands-on experience in different industries. One example is the Spokane Tribe of Indians' Summer Youth Employment Program in Washington State. Throughout the summer, tribal students ages fourteen to seventeen can gain work experience through jobs ranging from yard work to office work. They also attend STEM events hosted by colleges and universities.

> **"We're really trying to open their eyes to what's out there, things they've heard about but maybe didn't realize were real."[17]**
>
> **—Jewel Trujillo, program manager of the Spokane Tribe of Indians' Summer Youth Employment Program**

One such event took place in 2023. Students spent a day at Spokane Falls Community College. While there, they participated in advanced STEM activities, including working with cadavers as part of a medical science module. "We're really trying to open their eyes to what's out there, things they've heard about but maybe didn't realize were real,"[17] says Jewel Trujillo, the program supervisor. Programs like this are designed to spark students' curiosity and help them identify fields they might not have considered.

Other summer programs focus on a variety of career fields, including business, health care, technology, and the arts. Students can find opportunities through local community centers, nonprofit

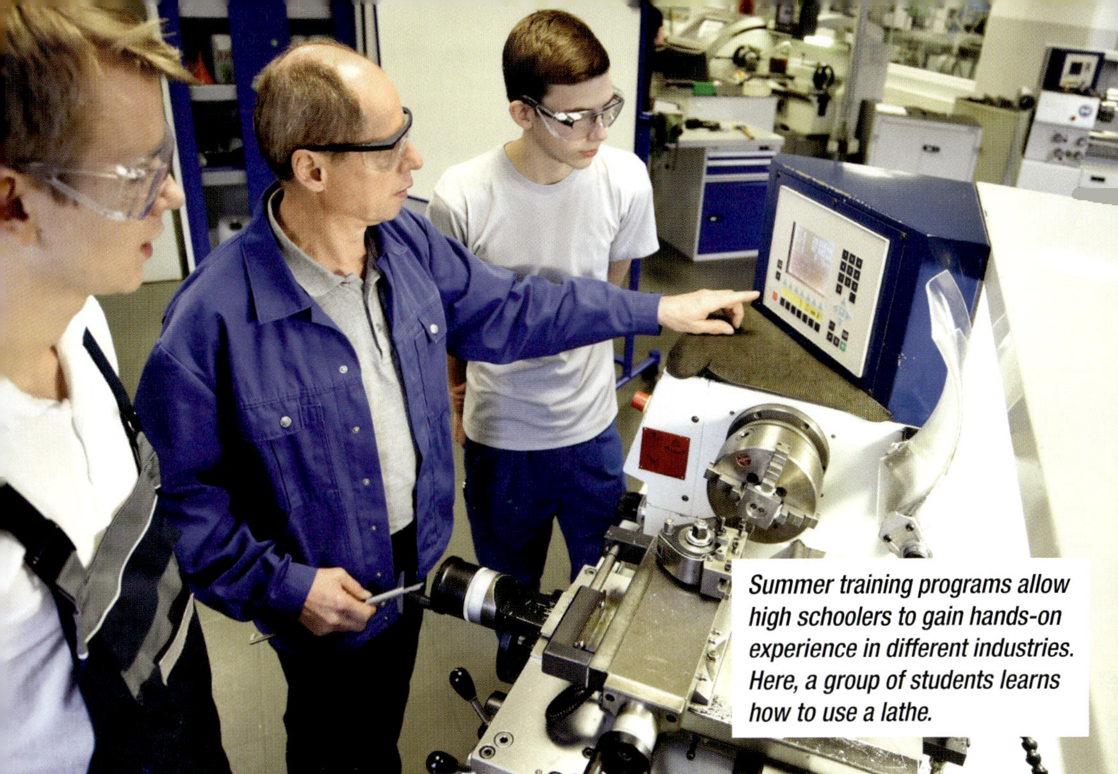
Summer training programs allow high schoolers to gain hands-on experience in different industries. Here, a group of students learns how to use a lathe.

organizations, and online resources. Participating in these programs allows students to interact with professionals in the field, ask questions, and gain firsthand knowledge of what working in a particular career is really like.

One example in Virginia is the Norfolk Emerging Leaders program, offered by the city government in the summer. This program, for high school and college students, provides leadership training and exposure to careers in local government and public service. The program offers students the chance to work on community projects, such as working as a recreation leader at the city's summer camps or as an aide at the city's senior centers. Through these projects, students gain valuable skills in communication, teamwork, and problem solving. The program provides paid summer employment for Norfolk youth ages sixteen to twenty-one and requires participants to agree to work thirty to forty hour per week. Participants gain hands-on work experience in various city departments, explore public service careers, and also receive job readiness training and financial literacy education.

Proactive

By using available resources, from online research to hands-on programs, you can explore a wide variety of career paths and gain valuable skills and experience. These resources can help you make informed decisions about your future. Career centers, summer programs, and community initiatives all offer unique opportunities to discover your passions and think about future career options. As Jewel Trujillo of the Spokane STEM program says, "A lot of these kids don't know what they're into."[18] But by taking advantage of the resources available to you, you can take steps to find out. You can be proactive in determining your future.

Education and Skill Building

At Cavelero Mid High School in Spokane, Washington, students are learning an important lesson about preparing for their future careers: the more skills you develop, the more options you create for yourself throughout your life. The school offers courses that expose students to skills needed in various careers and even provides opportunities to earn certifications sought by employers. For example, students can obtain a Microsoft Office Specialist (MOS) certification, a globally recognized credential, in programs such as Word, Excel, PowerPoint, Access, and Outlook.

Ellie Tredway was a student at Cavelero in 2023. She wrote at that time about how she expected to benefit from spending time and energy building skills. "Earning an MOS certification will be valuable to me," she explains, "because it will, one, show my determination, because they are not super easy to get, and then two, it will help me, when I'm trying to prove that I know how to use computers, and Microsoft Software."[19] Tredway and her classmates are focusing on these courses as a way to learn as much as they can, gain new skills, or become more proficient in skills they already have. Whether it is through certification programs like those at Cavelero, taking classes that will help you in future careers, or enrolling in programs that focus on career fields that interest you, each action you take exposes you to new knowledge and develops new skills. This will give you more options for the future.

Career Pathway Programs

Many high schools offer career pathway programs. These are typically four-year programs that prepare students for college coursework that will lead to careers in specified fields such as engineering and health care. Students in these programs take all of the usual classes required for graduation, along with a structured series of industry-specific courses. Career pathway programs often include a rigorous application process with requirements such as a high middle school grade point average (GPA), an interview, and testing.

Career pathway programs typically pair a set sequence of courses with hands-on experiences. In the Engineering Pathway program at Castro Valley High School in California, students take specialized engineering-focused courses such as Introduction to Engineering Design, Principles of Engineering, and Civil Engineering & Architecture. Additionally, they get hands-on experience with computer-aided design software, computerized milling machines, 3-D printers, and robotic technology. Students in this program

Career pathway programs typically pair a set sequence of courses with hands-on experiences in a specific industry, such as robotics or engineering.

also have the opportunity to apply for summer internships in their chosen field.

A similar type of program is available to students at Matthew Fontaine Maury High School in Norfolk, Virginia. Called the Medical and Health Specialties Program, it operates in partnership with Norfolk's Eastern Virginia Medical School. This program accepts students with high GPAs from middle school who have already taken at least one high school math and one high school science course. Once in this program, students are required to take two science courses a year. One such course is anatomy, a class that allows students to gain unique hands-on experience working in a cadaver lab. Other required courses include biology, chemistry, and electives such as sports medicine. Throughout their four years, students attend lectures by health care professionals in different fields and visit research laboratories at colleges. Upon completing the school's health career pathway program, students receive a white coat to honor their work toward a medical career. (In medical schools, graduates are presented with their first white coat, symbolizing their entry into the medical profession.) "The [white coat] really is like a symbol . . . that I'm really interested in medicine and . . . I'm putting my foot towards the right step,"[20] high school student Maria Luzaran said after receiving her white coat in 2019. Luzaran continued her educational journey at Washington and Lee University to study biochemistry, both prepared for and inspired by her coursework in high school.

> **"The [white coat] really is like a symbol . . . that I'm really interested in medicine and . . . I'm putting my foot towards the right step."[20]**
>
> —Maria Luzaran on finishing the medical program in high school

Career and Technical Education

Career and Technical Education (CTE) programs are another option for students who want to explore potential careers while developing practical skills. These programs can lead to industry-recognized certifications, college credits, and even associate's

Professional Credits in High School

Two high schools in San Antonio, Texas, are piloting a new program called Career Kickstart. The program was designed to help students explore career options, whether they plan to attend college or enter the workforce directly after high school. It was created by the College Board—the organization known for its Advanced Placement (AP) program and standardized college-readiness tests like the SAT. Career Kickstart aims to bring the academic rigor of AP courses to Career and Technical Education (CTE) classes.

Launched in the 2024–2025 school year, Career Kickstart started with two pilot courses: AP Networking Fundamentals and AP Cybersecurity Fundamentals. Like other AP classes, these two follow a standardized framework, provide specialized teacher training, and include end-of-course exams. Depending on their performance, students can earn college credit or professional certifications, which gives them an advantage as they move into higher education or the workforce.

Unlike traditional AP courses that focus on academic subjects like history or biology, Career Kickstart focuses on industry-specific skills and credentials. The program's goal is to provide students with practical, career-focused knowledge while maintaining high academic standards. The success of the pilot programs could lead to expansion to more schools, which would enhance CTE opportunities for students nationwide.

degrees—all of which give students a competitive edge in the job market or a head start in furthering their education. CTE courses combine academic instruction with technical training. Trina Pruitt, a contributor to the Texas nonprofit education organization We Go Public, describes the benefits of high school CTE programs when she says, "Public high school students have many individual interests, and school districts provide opportunities to obtain current technical skills in preparation for a wide range of in-demand and high-paying careers. High schoolers can gain college credit and/or achieve industry certification before they complete graduation requirements."[21]

The possibilities within CTE programs are wide-ranging. Most of these programs are organized into career clusters such as culinary arts, graphic arts, automotive technology, health science, manufacturing, and cybersecurity. Students who choose the culinary arts cluster, for instance, will take classes that prepare them for jobs as cooks, pastry chefs, or food service managers. Examples of such classes include introduction to culinary arts and food science. Students who choose the health science cluster will take classes that prepare them for jobs as certified nursing assistants, home health aides, or emergency medical technicians. Among the possible classes they may take are principles of health science and medical terminology. And students who choose the automotive technology cluster will take courses that ready them for jobs such as automotive mechanics, service technicians, or automotive service advisors. Their classes may include automotive service and chassis maintenance.

The benefits of participating in CTE programs extend beyond career planning. Students in these programs have shown higher levels of success at school. According to a report by Advance CTE, a national nonprofit that advocates for high-quality career and technical education, 78 percent of students who complete CTE programs pursue postsecondary education or advanced training within two years of graduating high school. The same report notes that high school students who complete at least two course credits in a career track have about a 95 percent graduation rate, which is about 10 percent higher than the national average.

> **"I love to cook for people, and you get so many certificates and learn a lot, like knife skills and communication, which is very important in business."[22]**
>
> —Luis Reyes on his Career and Technical Education program

CTE programs can serve different purposes. They can lead students toward careers they had never considered. CTE programs can be equally valuable to students who already know the direction they want to go. Luis Reyes, who studies culinary arts as part of a CTE program at Horry County public schools in South Carolina, says his classes are preparing him for his dream of owning a restaurant. "That's my passion. I love to cook for people, and you get so many certificates and learn a lot, like knife skills and communication, which is very important in business,"[22] Reyes says.

Apprenticeships

Apprenticeships also offer a unique opportunity to explore potential careers while still in school. Similar to CTE programs, apprenticeships combine academic instruction with hands-on, real-world experience. The difference is that the real-world experience includes actually working alongside professionals in the field to develop practical skills. These programs may even provide a paycheck, making it easier for teens to earn while they learn.

Getting started with an apprenticeship in high school is possible if students make use of available resources. By working with school counselors, community organizations, or even searching online, students can find opportunities that match their interests and aspirations. For example, many states have programs set up through school partnerships with companies in various industries. These industries range from health care and information technology (IT) to advanced manufacturing. One such program in Iowa, for instance, places high school students in welding apprenticeships at an industrial and agricultural equipment manufacturer.

An experienced welder looks on as an apprentice welds a seam. Apprenticeships combine academic instruction with hands-on, real-world experience.

Fashion Found

Rose Garcia, a 2022 graduate of Manteca High School in Manteca, California, discovered her interest in interior design through the school's Career Technical Education (CTE) program. In high school, out of curiosity, she enrolled in an introductory interior design class. She was fascinated by the subject. "I never imagined myself taking an interior design class when I was younger. . . . Little did I know that decision would alter my future plans and lead me toward a career in interior design."

The skills and knowledge Garcia gained from her CTE courses paved the way for her role as a visual stylist at Living Spaces, a furniture and décor store. She even won a company-wide display contest. Her design was then featured across all forty Living Spaces stores nationwide. Garcia credits her professional achievement to her high school experience in the CTE courses, which gave her a foundation of skills and knowledge needed in the design world.

Quoted in Manteca Unified School District, "Crafting Your Path," January 31, 2024. www.mantecausd.net.

Apprenticeships often provide more than skills. They also offer direction for those who are unsure about their future. As a high school senior, Austin Boop of York, Pennsylvania, felt lost whenever he thought about what to do after graduation. Many people urged him to plan on college, but that did not feel right for Boop. He had some interest in electricity, and a counselor persuaded him to consider an apprenticeship. "She challenged me to take a hard look at different industries," says Boop. "Without her resources, knowledge, and patience to learn what I was interested in, I would not be where I am today."[23] He started with an apprenticeship in electrical work at age seventeen and soon discovered that it was the right path for him.

The apprenticeship was not easy. Boop recalls that the hours were often long and the work hard, but he valued and was interested in what he was learning. After four years of apprenticeship, he opened his own electrical business. His business has grown over time—to the point that he has added seven employees.

An apprenticeship also led to a career for Braden McAlpine. Growing up in Manchester, New Hampshire, McAlpine often helped his grandmother maintain an apartment building she owned. Because of this experience, he knew he wanted to work in a trade—a skilled profession that includes hands on work. While still in high school, he took classes in carpentry, electrical, and masonry at a local technical center. He also took a heating, ventilation, and air-conditioning (HVAC) class at a nearby community college. That is when he realized HVAC was what interested him most. He enrolled in an HVAC pre-apprenticeship program, during which he trained at three different companies. In his senior year of high school, he was offered a full apprenticeship at one of the companies. His apprenticeship started after graduation in 2023. It involved installing heating and cooling units. He explains, "The whole apprenticeship path for me has been amazing. I knew I wanted to do something hands-on, and here I am."[24]

What makes apprenticeships so valuable for students like Boop and McAlpine is that they combine education and real-world experience. They allow high schoolers to try out careers before committing to them. And students have a head start on the skills they will need if they go into those careers.

College Programs

For students interested in more academic exploration of their interests, courses and programs outside of their schools are a possibility. For some, summer college courses can provide the extra exploration they are seeking. While in high school, Allison Fuller decided to take summer classes at the University of California, Santa Cruz (UCSC). Because she has loved the ocean since she was a child, she chose to take an introduction to oceanography class. "I decided to take summer classes at UCSC to deepen my understanding of my passions before graduating high school. I wanted to build confidence in my ability to handle college-level courses and ensure that I choose a major that truly aligns with my interests,"[25] Fuller explains. This experi-

"I decided to take summer classes at UCSC to deepen my understanding of my passions before graduating high school."[25]

—Allison Fuller, high school student

Summer college courses provide academic enrichment while helping students to explore their interests and experience the college environment.

ence gave her a head start to see whether she was both academically suited and personally interested in pursuing a major and career focused on the ocean.

Another valuable aspect of outside courses is the opportunity to connect with college students. Engaging with those already in college can provide insights that you would not get otherwise. Eli Foraker, who also took a 2024 summer course at UCSC, talked with her college-age classmates about their college experience. “Don’t be afraid to talk to the other students already in college,” Foraker says. “I was a little nervous at first, but by the end, it was really helpful to be able to discuss things with everyone else.”[26] Conversations like these provide useful insights for high school students preparing to take their next steps.

For some students, study-away trips (which blend education and cultural enrichment) are another way to explore careers and get real-world experience. In 2019, high school student Katja Ziemer of St. Petersburg, Florida, took part in a weeklong archaeology study-away program in Canada. “In Montreal there is a museum—Pointe-à-Callière—that focuses on the city’s history and is located on the site of Montreal's first European settlement," Ziemer writes of her trip. "On this archaeological site, you can see remains of a fire, the outline of where the perimeter fence used to be, and the walls of the homes. As a lover of archaeology this was one of my favorite activities of the trip."[27] She says that the trip affirmed her passion for archaeology and reinforced her choice to follow this path as a career.

There are many ways students can investigate career possibilities while in high school. Often these pursuits also provide experience and skills that are valuable no matter what path the students follow. Using the resources available, students can gain a clearer sense of what they want for their future.

Building a Professional Network

It is never too early to start building a professional network. Networking—building relationships with people who can help you learn about careers, provide guidance, and connect you with job opportunities—is a crucial skill. At its core, networking is about talking to people. Networking can include asking questions. It can include stating your interests. It can include asking for help. The thing about networking is that you never know when a new contact will offer a meaningful connection or a new lead or help with developing an idea.

Charles Nyabeze discovered the power of networking at a young age. In 2020, during his final year of high school, Nyabeze cofounded a cryptocurrency platform. For a few years before that, he had been interested in the idea of starting his own business. He had never really talked about this with anyone, until one day he started talking with a classmate while the two were washing their hands in the high school restroom. Within days the two students had joined with other classmates who were involved in creating the crypto platform. Their project was so successful that it was eventually bought by another company for a large chunk of money. This was a classic example of how just talking to someone about your ideas can sometimes lead to new career ventures. That is the essence of networking. As Nyabeze notes, "You never know, the guy washing his hands next to you in the washroom could be your next best friend or future business partner."[28]

> "You never know, the guy washing his hands next to you in the washroom could be your next best friend or future business partner."[28]
>
> —Charles Nyabeze, cofounder of a cryptocurrency platform

There are other benefits to networking. By talking to people in different professions, you can learn a great deal about the work being done in those fields. Networking can also help you connect with a mentor—someone who agrees to guide and assist your effort to decide on a career or find a job. Hannah Magino, a high school senior in Maryland, explains, "Relationships are a fundamental part of life and the basis of networking. It's crucial to start building these relationships from a young age. The people you meet and bond with in high school are the ones you can ask for advice and help with SAT preparation, referrals for jobs, recommendation letters for scholarships and college, and much more."[29]

Where to Start?

The idea of networking may seem daunting. How should you begin to make these connections? It starts with talking to people you know and asking questions. Consider the network you already have—your family, friends, and school community. Ask

Networking begins with the people who are already in your circle, such as friends, family, and teachers.

Benefits of School Mentors

A mentor doesn't need to work in the career you're pursuing or interested in. Mentors guide, inspire, and help you navigate your path by sharing valuable advice and connecting you with resources. Establishing a mentorship relationship with teachers, coaches, and other school staff can be a great choice even if you're not planning to become an educator. They can support your academic and career goals by offering encouragement, helping with recommendations, and connecting you to relevant opportunities. A 2021 study by EdWeek Research Center explored the mentor relationship between students and middle and high school staff. Researchers used data from teens across the United States and found that 54 percent of students considered a teacher a mentor, and 41 percent responded that a school counselor was their mentor. Additionally, a 2023 study from the National Bureau of Economic Research found that those with mentors were 9.4 percent more likely to attend college. Among this group, according to the study, students from lower-income families experienced the biggest boost. The study confirmed that mentoring by school personnel can result in positive steps toward a student's future.

about their jobs, their volunteer experiences, and their community involvement. Share any experiences that interest you, and let them know about your personal passions.

Networking is not merely about collecting contacts or asking for favors; it's about building meaningful relationships where both parties can learn and grow. When you approach networking as an opportunity to connect and share experiences, you develop skills that benefit your academic, social, and professional life. Genuine relationships often lead to authentic opportunities because of the trust and respect built over time.

Magino highlights how even casual connections in a school setting can open doors: "For example, the upperclassman who sat next to you in math may have noticed how good you are at explaining topics they don't understand," she writes. "As your friend, they may recommend you for a job at a tutoring center. They may even know the boss and be able to put in a good word for you. The jobs you get can lead you to more fantastic opportunities."[30] Real relationships can result in unexpected career pathways.

Through Clubs

Students can form these types of relationships by joining organizations and clubs. Doing so allows you to pursue your interests while also connecting with peers and professionals who have similar interests. Student organizations and school clubs are a good place to start.

One such organization is Junior Achievement. Each year, the organization holds a national competition that requires high school students to form real businesses, create products or services, and secure investors. During this process they receive help and advice from business professionals. The top student businesses are then chosen to showcase their work at the National Student Leadership Summit in Washington, DC. The summit is attended by business leaders and members of Congress. Fifteen student teams took part in the summit in 2022. The process of creating their businesses, presenting them to attendees, and talking about their projects with other students and with business professionals and

Students work on a listening skills activity while attending the Student Leadership Summit in St. Petersburg, Florida on January 25, 2023.

members of Congress leads to many opportunities for valuable interaction. “It was a great experience to meet other students from all over the country and further grow my network,” says Rachel, one of the participants. “I could expand on my entrepreneurial ideas and learn from others’ advice and stories.”[31]

> **“It was a great experience to meet other students from all over the country and further grow my network. I could expand on my entrepreneurial ideas and learn from others’ advice and stories.”[31]**
>
> **—Rachel, high school finalist at Junior Achievement National Student Leadership Summit competition**

School clubs also offer a place to build relationships with peers and professionals. At Coronado Middle School in California, students in the Robotics Club have formed meaningful connections with both groups. During a 2024 visit to the US Navy’s robotics division, students explored unmanned underwater vehicles (UUVs) and engaged with navy engineers eager to share their expertise. Robotics mentor Kevin Ward reflects, “Talking to some of these engineers with the Navy who showed us the UUVs, they were so excited and so happy to talk about what they do. They were thrilled to be working with our kids and to have that connection.”[32]

Ward also highlighted how the club fosters lasting peer relationships. He shared the story of a former team member who moved to Boston but continues collaborating with the group. Despite the distance, current and former members of the group stay in contact, share technical knowledge, and maintain friendships formed through the program. Clubs like this one create supportive networks that extend beyond the classroom and even across the country.

Mentors in the Community

Another effective way to develop and expand a network is through mentorship. Finding a mentor can seem challenging, but students can find one through family contacts, school programs, and community organizations. If interested in a specific field, students can use these contacts to meet someone in that field. At this point, teens can start a relationship by asking questions about the field, education, and career paths. The key is to establish a relationship in which one can learn and seek advice.

ACE Mentor Program of America is a free after-school mentoring program for high school students who have an interest in careers in architecture, construction, and engineering. ACE serves students across the United States. It has four thousand mentors working with over ten thousand students each year. ACE mentorship was pivotal in Emma Blanchard's journey to an engineering career. She joined the program as a high school sophomore. The people she has connected with through the program have inspired her, provided advice, and helped her find opportunities to explore. "Through ACE, I met some inspirational engineers who convinced me to join the engineering field," Blanchard explains. "During college, they reached out to me to help review my résumé and recommended I apply for an internship at their company. Through that internship, I confirmed my love of construction management and pursued a career in construction management."[33] In 2024 Blanchard was working as an assistant project manager at a construction company in Maryland. Wanting to help other students the way she had been helped, she is now also volunteering as a mentor through the same organization.

> **"During college, [the ACE mentors] reached out to me to help review my résumé and recommended I apply for an internship at their company."[33]**
>
> —Emma Blanchard, mentee and mentor with ACE Mentor Program of America

Online Platforms

Social media platforms can also be a tool for developing a professional network. LinkedIn is a well-known professional networking platform. On LinkedIn, you build professional connections by creating a profile to showcase your skills, education, and experiences. This profile can be used to interest potential employers. You can search for key words to discover career opportunities, internships, and connect with people in fields you're interested in. By connecting with professionals, you can explore careers and gain valuable insights.

Social media platforms can be tools for developing a professional network. LinkedIn users create profiles to showcase their skills, education, and experiences.

Creating a LinkedIn profile is easy. You start by signing up with a professional-sounding email address, adding a clear photo in clothes appropriate for a job interview, and writing a headline that highlights your potential career interests, such as Aspiring Photographer. In the summary section, share your goals, achievements, and relevant experiences, including part-time jobs or school projects.

Building an online network begins with reaching out to people you already know. Start by sending connection requests to parents, teachers, mentors, coaches, and other adults familiar with you. Include individuals who might write recommendations for college or jobs in the future. Engage actively with your network by liking, commenting on, and sharing relevant posts to foster connections. When reaching out to professionals, personalize your messages by referencing shared interests or how you came across their work.

Studies have found that career platforms such as LinkedIn help students explore their future work options. In 2023 journalist Anya Kamenetz looked at how teens use LinkedIn for career development. One of the students she interviewed was Nora, a first-year student at Yale University. Nora shared that she joined LinkedIn at age sixteen to stay updated on topics like artificial intelligence by connecting with others who post and discuss related content. Another student, Zachary, emphasized LinkedIn's value for finding internships and jobs by following posts from company representatives. He noted that the platform provided opportunities he otherwise wouldn't have discovered.

Different Ways to Network

There are many different ways to network, and sometimes they yield surprising results. William Beguhn, for example, grew up on Kwajalein, an island in the Marshall Islands, where one of his favorite activities was scuba diving. As much as he enjoyed diving, his time underwater exposed him to the damaging effects of climate change on coral reefs. This experience inspired him to pursue a career focused on preserving and protecting natural ecosystems.

When Beguhn's family moved to Concord, New Hampshire, during his teenage years, he began considering ways to connect with people and organizations dedicated to environmental conservation. Hoping to find guidance and opportunities, he took the initiative to reach out online. "I spent several months researching, sending emails, talking to anyone who would listen, and finally, I found Minuteman National Historical Park,"[34] Beguhn says.

In 2018, after connecting with the park, Beguhn began volunteering there during his summer break from high school. Volunteering is another way to add people to your network. It gives you a chance to learn new skills. It is also a good way to meet people and learn about the work they do. At the park, Beguhn's volunteer work included pulling weeds, sweeping, and mopping. But he also talked to park employees and learned about a whole range of other jobs. His efforts paid off, as he eventually got a

Informational Interviews

High school students can expand their professional network by conducting informational interviews. An informational interview is a meeting in which you ask someone working in a career you're interested in learning about how they got started, what they do, and what skills are needed for it. These conversations can help you learn about different career paths and build valuable contacts. Start by identifying professionals through family, teachers, or local businesses. Do not feel intimidated about contacting them. People generally enjoy talking about themselves as well as helping students who show initiative. Reach out politely by calling or emailing to explain your interest in their career and ask whether they could spare ten to fifteen minutes to talk. Prepare thoughtful questions beforehand, such as, "What do you enjoy most about your job?" or "What skills should I develop to succeed in this field?" The interview does not need to lead directly to a job or internship. Instead, the point is to build your confidence, make a lasting impression, and learn more about a particular career field. Professionals often appreciate the chance to share their experiences and could keep you in mind for future opportunities. Afterward, follow up with a thank-you message or note expressing appreciation for the time they spent talking with you.

summer internship at the park. The internship included inspecting and taking care of the park's landscapes. This experience reinforced his passion for environmental preservation and brought him closer to his goal of working in that field as a career.

Teens like Beguhn have discovered that networking can significantly enhance a person's career aims. Building relationships with individuals in your areas of interest can provide valuable connections, guidance, and potential opportunities. Establishing these connections helps create a supportive network that can open doors to future careers, internships, and mentorships.

Being Flexible in Your Career Path

Reem Elsaad thought she had her future all figured out when she chose biomedical engineering as her major at Arizona State University. She believed it was her passion and would lead her to a fulfilling career. However, during her second semester of college, she realized her feelings had changed. "There are many reasons why I ended up changing, but ultimately, it was because I could not see myself working as a biomedical engineer. I lost interest in the material I was studying, and I wasn't able to fully engage in classes or enjoy college life,"[35] Elsaad writes.

> "There are many reasons why I ended up changing [my major], but ultimately, it was because I could not see myself working as a biomedical engineer. I lost interest in the material I was studying and I wasn't able to fully engage in classes or enjoy college life."[35]
>
> —Reem Elsaad, Arizona State University graduate

After this realization, Elsaad decided to explore different classes and not declare a major. She then took a course that focused on exploring different majors and careers, and she considered her personality and interests. Based on this, Elsaad switched her major to political science at the end of her freshman year. It was a good choice. She got a position as a management and administrative intern for the mayor's office in Tempe, Arizona, in the summer of 2022. She graduated college with majors in political science and global studies. In 2024

Elsaad began working as the executive assistant to Arizona's assistant secretary of state.

Elsaad understood how important it is to be open to change in your career journey, especially in a world that's constantly evolving. New technologies, global events, and shifting personal interests mean career paths aren't always straight lines. Being flexible is how you stay ready for whatever comes next.

New Skills Lead to a New Path

Careers today are more unpredictable than ever. According to the Bureau of Labor Statistics, most people change jobs about twelve times in their professional careers. People change jobs for many reasons. One reason is that technological advancements can eliminate the need for certain jobs but create demand for new ones. As a result, new types of jobs are becoming available each year. For example, jobs like app developers or social media managers did not exist a few decades ago but are prevalent today. Staying open to change can lead to exciting opportunities.

Katie Sheridan started her professional life as a middle school English teacher in Herndon, Virginia. Although she enjoyed her work, over time she developed a strong interest in emerging digital technologies. She realized that the latest applications could help her teach more effectively. At the time, most teachers were sticking to traditional methods, but Sheridan learned Google Docs, Slides, and Sheets to simplify her work and enhance learning. Using the advanced features these applications offered, she created interactive digital lessons incorporating dynamic tools like drag-and-drop activities, sorting exercises, and educational video games. This approach proved invaluable when the COVID-19 pandemic hit, allowing Sheridan to deliver engaging lessons in a fully digital environment. This led to the realization that working with technology excited her more than teaching.

Sheridan did not change her career right away. She had devoted a decade to teaching but eventually realized her zeal for teaching had waned. At the same time, she noticed the growing

During the COVID-19 pandemic, the move to digital schooling forced educators to use technology in new ways. For some, this change inspired new career paths.

influence of technology and artificial intelligence, inspiring in her a desire to pursue technology professionally. "I watched the trends grow for technology via AI, ChatGPT, etc. I knew I had to get in on this, not just as a career move, but as a way to study something I wanted to know more about,"[36] explains Sheridan.

Sheridan enrolled in a rigorous tech boot camp to learn more about coding and technology. She experienced self-doubt, especially when she struggled with difficult coursework and failed some of the exams. However, Sheridan pushed through it. She learned from her failures. She built strong troubleshooting skills and developed a passion for problem solving.

> "I watched the trends grow for technology via AI, ChatGPT, etc. I knew I had to get in on this, not just as a career move, but as a way to study something I wanted to know more about."[36]
>
> —Katie Sheridan, former teacher

After putting in a lot of work, Sheridan passed the course. In 2023 she started a new job as a cloud innovation specialist. She is happy in her new career but has learned to always be open to change. "In the end," she writes, "my 'why' is whatever is driving my passions. And, as that changes over time, I think it's important to always follow whatever path is bringing you the most happiness. Sometimes it takes a knee-jerk reaction to get you out of the rut you're in. In my case, it was professionally. I went out of my comfort zone and made a change."[37]

Realizations

Like Sheridan, Arthur Littmann changed his career plans as he learned more about himself and what he found interesting. While in college, Littmann studied business and marketing mainly because he was unsure what to major in. As he got closer to graduation, he realized that the idea of working in business didn't excite him. "I kept thinking that if anyone hired me, all I'd be bringing to the table is an extra pair of hands that could answer the phone and fill Excel spreadsheets,"[38] Littmann recalls.

Finding Greatness

Many successful people found greatness after taking unexpected career detours. Vera Wang, now a world-famous fashion designer, did not start out in fashion. She pursued figure skating and journalism before switching careers at age forty. Her decision to follow her creative passion led her to build one of the most iconic bridal design brands in the world. Similarly, Dwayne "the Rock" Johnson dreamed of being a professional football player but was cut from the Canadian Football League. Facing disappointment, he turned to wrestling, becoming a World Wrestling Entertainment superstar. "I had been sulking on the sofa just watching trashy TV until that point," Johnson says of his time after being cut. "I decided there and then that, even if it wasn't in football, the world was still going to hear from me. That's pretty much where my wrestling career started." Eventually, he changed course again, launching a successful acting career and becoming one of Hollywood's highest-paid actors.

These stories show that career paths aren't always straight lines—and that's okay. Flexibility and willingness to explore new passions can open doors you may not have considered.

Quoted in Jake Thompson, "Dwayne 'the Rock' Johnson's Most Inspirational Quotes on Life, Family, Success & Giving Back," E! Online, December 4, 2021. www.eonline.com.

After graduation, Littmann followed the business route because he was unsure of what else to do. He found an internship that put his business degree to use, but he soon discovered the work was exactly what he had expected. During an internship at a start-up in Paris, he spent his time answering calls and filling out spreadsheets, tasks that felt mundane to him. He was much more interested in the work of the product team—developers, designers, and product managers—who build and maintain the company's core products. For example, Littmann was intrigued as he watched the developers prototype an app in just two weeks. This made him realize he wanted to change paths to a career in IT.

Littmann didn't have the skills to pursue a job in IT. He was even offered a full-time job as a sales manager, utilizing his business degree, which he considered. But he knew that if he took the job, he would likely stay in that career for a long time—and likely not enjoy it. So he took a chance. He turned down the job, moved to London, and took a nine-week coding course. Having successfully completed the course, Littmann got a job in the IT field and as of 2024 was working as a senior software lead for a London-based company. Taking the chance and putting in the work to follow his interests allowed him to develop a career that excited him.

Changing Majors

Some people realize as early as college that the road they are following is not the one for them. It is natural for a person's interests to evolve with new experiences. Many teens go to college or start a job right out of high school, confident in their path, but later discover other subjects or pursuits that are better suited for them. In fact, according to the National Center for Education Statistics, around 80 percent of US college students change their major at least once.

Having a goal when attending college is positive—it helps with focus and drive. At the same time, it is important to be open to the possibility that your interests may change. Emily Ravet was in her junior year at the University of Wisconsin–Madison when

Around 80 percent of US college students change their major at least once. A student who starts out as an engineering major may find themselves in journalism as their interests evolve.

she realized she wanted to change course in her career goals. She had started with the idea of going into marketing, but she struggled with one class in her major. At the same time, she discovered that she enjoyed a journalism class—and excelled at it. Realizing that her true passion and skill were tied to storytelling, she switched to a journalism major.

Change is not easy. For Ravet, the change required taking six extra courses outside of her regular semesters. This meant she had to spend more money and time on school than initially planned. However, she knew it was the right decision in the long term. "This decision did cost me money, but now I am working a job that I love and have zero regrets about switching my major so late in the game,"[39] Ravet reflects. She graduated with a degree in journalism and got a job as a content strategist for a tech start-up company.

The key is to never feel you are stuck in one field, no matter what stage of life you are in. At most colleges and universities, students can change their majors until they find the right one,

> "Some students change their major six times before finding their perfect fit!"[40]
>
> —Emily Ravet, University of Wisconsin–Madison graduate

and even then, they do not have to follow that particular path once they graduate. "Some students change their major six times before finding their perfect fit!" writes Ravet. "Just because you majored in a topic, you don't have to work in that field. Many adults do not work in the topic that they majored in. Once you break into the job market, experience is the most important thing, not what you majored in."[40]

Growth Mindset

Being able to embrace change means recognizing when you need to change—and then giving yourself space to adapt. Adapting doesn't mean you're giving up; it means growing, learning, and realigning your goals. A major way to do this is by developing a growth mindset as a teen.

Notable psychologist Carol Dweck's research on the growth mindset highlights how embracing new challenges can lead to greater personal and professional development. A growth mindset is the belief that one's abilities can be developed through dedication and hard work. This mindset leads to resilience and a love of learning, allowing individuals to grow and change. People with a growth mindset view challenges, such as a change in major or career, as opportunities to grow, rather than obstacles. By focusing on effort and learning from failures, individuals can achieve long-term success, regardless of changes in themselves or their environment.

Developing a growth mindset includes embracing challenges, staying curious, and learning from setbacks. Teens can start by stepping outside their comfort zones—whether by trying a new hobby, joining a new club, or tackling a difficult subject in school. When faced with criticism, teens should focus on what they can improve rather than feeling discouraged. Setting realistic goals—like studying for an hour each day for a difficult class—helps maintain motivation. Additionally, practicing self-reflection by keeping a

Practicing self-reflection by keeping a journal of achievements and lessons learned from setbacks can reinforce a positive attitude toward growth.

journal of achievements and lessons learned from setbacks can reinforce a positive attitude toward growth. By staying open to feedback and seeing mistakes as learning opportunities, teens can build resilience, which will allow them to see change as a positive in their careers.

While a student at Central College in Iowa, Jaime Miranda experienced a turning point. Miranda's life had included many struggles, including living in and out of homeless shelters and his mother dying of cancer. While Miranda made it to college, he struggled soon after arriving. He did not feel connected to his peers. He faced major difficulties with academics and started failing his classes. It was his wrestling coach who encouraged him to develop a growth mindset to deal with the difficulties. Rather than taking the negative feedback about Miranda's struggles in his classes as an indicator of a lack of ability or intelligence, his coach told him to see it as a behavior he could overcome. When Miranda was faced with failing grades, his wrestling coach said, "School is hard. So what? It's hard for a lot of people. They figured it out. You can figure it out, too."[41] This perspective shift motivated Miranda to seek help from professors and tutors, which led to improved grades and increased confidence in his academic abilities. He turned all of his Fs into Ds and eventually Cs—finally passing all of his classes.

The positive mindset also helped him adjust to other aspects of his life. He started reaching out and feeling accepted by his teammates and became more confident in both his academics and his wrestling. After college, he enlisted in the US Marines, and following an active-duty tour, he became a teacher and a high school wrestling coach. Then in 2024 he joined the Central College staff as an assistant women's wrestling coach. As he em-

Lifelong Learning

Realizing the importance of continuing to learn throughout your life will allow you to more easily adjust when change is needed. Eduardo Briceño, a leadership expert, explains that many people start their careers eager to learn, but as they gain experience, they think they've learned all they need to know. This type of thinking can block new opportunities. Briceño says:

> When we graduate college and start our careers, we often understand that we have a lot to learn, so we approach our jobs with a learning orientation. We ask questions; we observe others; we know we may be wrong; and we realize we're works in progress. But once we gain competence in our jobs, too many of us stop learning and growing. The most successful people—in work and in life—never stop deliberately continuing to learn and improve.

Lifelong learners constantly challenge themselves, whether by mastering a new skill, earning additional certifications, or exploring emerging trends in their fields. This keeps people adaptable and ready for any changes that might come.

Quoted in Rebekah Barnett, "What Advice Do You Wish You'd Gotten When You Graduated from College? 25 TED Speakers Answer," TED.com, May 22, 2018. https://ideas.ted.com.

braced the idea that skills can be developed through effort and persistence, Miranda transformed his approach to learning and equipped himself for his future.

Miranda's attitude prepared him not just for a changing career but for life, which has its twists and turns. Flexibility, resilience, and a willingness to learn will keep you moving forward—often toward something better than you initially planned. Getting ready for your future career means staying curious and adaptable to life's unexpected turns.

Introduction: Building Your Future

1. Quoted in *Smithsonian*, "The Future Is Bright If More Teens Could Think About High School the Way Kavya Kopparapu Does," 2025. www.smithsonianmag.com.
2. Katherine Kemmeries Cecala, "Why Career Exploration Needs to Start Much Sooner for Students," Junior Achievement Arizona, November 13, 2024. www.jaaz.org.
3. Quoted in Habitat for Humanity, "Student Volunteers Develop Trade Skills on Build Sites," 2025. www.habitat.org.

Chapter One: Understanding Yourself—Discovering Interests, Skills, and Values

4. Quoted in Birkman, "Why Career Assessments Are Critical for Teens and College Students," 2025. https://birkman.com.
5. Quoted in Birkman, "Why Career Assessments Are Critical for Teens and College Students."
6. Quoted in Rajan Chitrao, "Alumni Spotlight: MacKenzie Perez," DECA Direct, February 7, 2022. www.decadirect.org.
7. Jake Christianson, "How My HS Helped Me Find My Career Path When I Realized College Wasn't for Me," 74 Million, October 2, 2024. www.the74million.org.
8. Quoted in Bernardo Frias, "MacArthur Student Finds Success with Computer Science, Paving the Way for Other Girls," The Insider, April 10, 2024. https://theinsider.irvingisd.net.
9. Quoted in Katherine Clifford, "How Amanda Gorman Used Writing to Overcome a Speech Impediment," CNBC, January 1, 2021. www.cnbc.com.
10. Quoted in Because of Them, We Can, "2023 'Young Frontrunner' Honoree Nupol Kiazolu Is on the Frontlines Pushing Us Forward," 2023. www.becauseofthemwecan.com.
11. Sebastian Rosero-Mayer, "Looking Back at My High School Journey and Looking Forward to the Future: A Personal Account," Science Survey, July 21, 2023. https://thesciencesurvey.com.

Chapter Two: Research, Resources, and the Real World

12. Korey Busby, "About," LinkedIn. www.linkedin.com.
13. Laure Depaty, "The Importance of Internships for High School Students," *Academics* (blog), EF Academy, 2019. www.ef.com.

14. Andrew Cruz, "My Experience as a High School Intern at Lockheed Martin," Medium, August 1, 2023. https://medium.com.
15. Quoted in UCLA Health, "Read Volunteer Testimonials," 2024. www.uclahealth.org.
16. Quoted in Shannon Doyne, "Should All High School Students Have Part-Time Jobs?," *New York Times*, September 22, 2022. www.nytimes.com.
17. Quoted in Elena Perry, "Youth from Spokane Tribe Learn from Cadavers Through Employment Program at SFCC," *Spokane (WA) Spokesman-Review*, August 10, 2023. www.spokesman.com.
18. Quoted in Perry, "Youth from Spokane Tribe Learn from Cadavers Through Employment Program at SFCC."

Chapter Three: Education and Skill Building

19. Quoted in Certiport, *MOS Success Story Cavelero Mid High School*, YouTube, October 16, 2023. www.youtube.com/watch?v=97_wl2cc6cE.
20. Quoted in Facebook, "Maury Medical Students Receive White Coats," January 9, 2019. www.facebook.com.
21. Trina Pruitt, "160 High School CTE Programs," We Go Public, March 1, 2020. www.wegopublic.com.
22. Quoted in Savannah Denton, "Horry County Schools Kicks Off Second Career Readiness Showcase with Partnership Grand Strand," Yahoo!, October 23, 2024. www.yahoo.com.
23. Quoted in Mark Perna, "From Apprentice to Entrepreneur: 'Apprenticeship Changed My Life,'" *Forbes*, November 10, 2020. www.forbes.com.
24. Quoted in Apprenticeship USA, "Helping His Grandmother Led to an HVAC Career," May 7, 2024. www.apprenticeship.gov.
25. Quoted in UC Santa Cruz, "High School Stories," 2024. https://summer.ucsc.edu.
26. Quoted in UC Santa Cruz, "High School Stories."
27. Katja Ziemer, "SPC High School Student Affirms Her Passion for Archaeology in Canada," St. Petersburg College, 2019. https://blog.spcollege.edu.

Chapter Four: Building a Professional Network

28. Charles Nyabeze, "The Value of Networking as a Teen: 10 Ways to Make Meaningful Connection with the Right Here," Future North, November 24, 2021. https:// futurenorth.ca.

29. Hannah Magino, "Why Networking in High School Is More Important than You Think," Simply Soft Skills, 2025. https://simplysoftskills.org.
30. Magino, "Why Networking in High School Is More Important than You Think."
31. Quoted in Burton D. Morgan Foundation, "Reflections from Junior Achievement Competition Finalists," July 19, 2022. www.bdmorganfdn.org.
32. Quoted in Brooke Clifford, "Hands-On Learning Leads to Big Successes for CMS Robotics Program," *Coronado (CA) Eagle & Journal*, October 26, 2021. www.coronadonewsca.com.
33. Quoted in LinkedIn, "ACE Mentor Program of America," 2024. www.linkedin.com.
34. Quoted in TEDx Talks, *Taking Action in High School Through Networking*, YouTube 2019. www.youtube.com/watch?v=MllznlrXD9I.

Chapter 5: Being Flexible in Your Career Path

35. Reem Elsaad, "I Changed My Major and Here's Why," *Hey Sunny* (blog), Arizona State University. https://heysunny.asu.edu.
36. Katie Sheridan, "My Career Switch to Tech: Remembering My Why," Medium, July 28, 2023. https://medium.com.
37. Sheridan, "My Career Switch to Tech."
38. Arthur Littmann, "How Learning to Code Has Changed My Life: My Story Two Years On," Medium, November 14, 2018. https://medium.com.
39. Emily Ravet, "5 Things to Think About Before Changing Your College Major," Universities.com, May 28, 2023. www.universities.com.
40. Ravet, "5 Things to Think About Before Changing Your College Major."
41. Quoted in Larry Happell and Chris Hulleman, "Three Mindset Shifts that Can Help Students Succeed," *Greater Good*, November 21, 2019. https://greatergood.berkeley.edu.

Books

Carol Christen, *What Color Is Your Parachute? For Teens: Discover Yourself, Design Your Future, and Plan for Your Dream Job*. Berkeley, CA: Ten Speed, 2022.

Richard Meadows, *The Essential Career Planning Handbook for Teens*. Self-published, 2023.

Peterson's Publishing, *Teens' Guide to College and Career Planning*. New York: Peterson's, 2022.

Nicholas Suivski, *Life After High School: A Teen Guide to Career Planning*. Minneapolis: Twenty-First Century, 2024.

Diane P. Tuccilo, *The Teen Library Internship Handbook*. Lanham, MD: Rowman & Littlefield, 2021.

Internet Sources

Annie E. Casey Foundation, "The Benefits of Workforce Exposure and Career Programming for Youth and Young Adults," May 2, 2021. www.aecf.org.

Apprenticeship.gov, "Youth Apprenticeship: A Career Pathway for Students," September 10, 2024. www.apprenticeship.gov.

Katie Arnoult, "Opinion: Why Every Teen Should Volunteer," Spotlight Schools, December 11, 2024. www.spotlightschools.com.

ASVAB Career Exploration Program, "First Job Work Experience," December 13, 2024. www.asvabprogram.com.

Dallin Cooper, "How to Find Your Passion in High School." https://dallincooper.com.

Catherine Garcia, "New York Teens Become EMTs to Solve Shortage in Their Town," The Week, February 18, 2022. https://theweek.com.

Indeed, "Interview Tips for Teens," August 18, 2024. www.indeed.com.

Indeed, "21 Useful Internship Tips for Career Success," July 25, 2024. www.indeed.com.

Organizations

Association for Career and Technical Education (ACTE)
www.acteonline.org
The ACTE is a valuable resource for teens interested in career and technical education. It provides information on various career pathways,

technical skills training, and industry certifications. Teens can explore career clusters and learn how to prepare for future jobs through educational programs and internships.

BigFuture
https://bigfuture.collegeboard.org
The BigFuture website, part of the College Board, helps teens navigate college and career planning. It offers tools for researching colleges, exploring career options, and planning financial aid. It includes career and college quizzes to help determine what teens are best suited for based on their interests and skills. Teens can create personalized plans using the tools on the website.

Bureau of Labor Statistics (BLS)
www.bls.gov
The BLS offers detailed job market data, including salary expectations, required skills, and job outlooks for hundreds of careers. Teens can use the *Occupational Outlook Handbook* to explore careers by industry, educational level, or projected growth.

CareerAddict
www.careeraddict.com
CareerAddict provides career advice on topics such as choosing a profession, writing résumés, and preparing for job interviews. It features career guides, job search tips, and skill-building resources aimed at helping teens and young adults succeed professionally.

MENTOR
www.mentoring.org
MENTOR focuses on connecting young people with mentors who can guide them in their academic and career journeys. Its website provides resources on finding mentoring programs and advice on building strong mentoring relationships. It provides stories of those who have mentored and been mentored.

VolunteerMatch
www.volunteermatch.org
VolunteerMatch connects teens with volunteer opportunities tailored to their skills and career interests. Volunteering can help teens gain real-world experience, develop professional skills, and strengthen college or job applications while making a positive impact in their communities. The website allows people to search for volunteer opportunities in their area.

INDEX

Note: Boldface page numbers indicate illustrations.

PICTURE CREDITS

Cover: Makistock/Shutterstock

6: Monkey Business Images/Shutterstock
9: Ground Picture/Shutterstock
12: Jannis Tobias Werner/Shutterstock
14: Oleksandr Lysenko/Shutterstock
18: FotoAndalucia/Shutterstock
21: VH-studio/Shutterstock
25: ALPA PROD/Shutterstock
28: SeventyFour/Shutterstock
32: Wirestock Creators/Shutterstock
35: Richard Levine/Alamy Stock Photo
38: New Jadsada/Shutterstock
40: antoniodiaz/Shutterstock
43: ViDI Studio/Shutterstock
48: Srdjan Randjelovic/Shutterstock
51: Jasminko Ibrakovic/Shutterstock
53: Akira AB November8/Shutterstock

ABOUT THE AUTHOR

Leanne Currie-McGhee has written books for the past two decades. She lives in Norfolk, Virginia, with her husband, Keith, daughters, Grace and Sol, and their dog, Delilah.